Identity Theft
THE PERSONAL GUIDE

COLD HARD REALITY

Mark A Priganc

Version: 2.1

Published by: Lulu Enterprises Inc.
860 Aviation Parkway, Suite 300
Morrisville, NC 27560 USA

ISBN 978-1-4357-0362-9

Photo Credits:

Chris Malloch, Stock.xchng, DHS, DOJ, FBI, FTC, Gunka Designs, AarinFreePhotos.com

Cover Design and Layout by Chris Malloch with GUNKA® Designs.

E-mail: author@IdentityTheft-Reality.com

Table of Contents

About the Author   8

What is Identity Theft?   10

You Will Be a Victim   12

Identity Theft Takes Many Forms: 17

     Drivers License Identity Theft   19
     Social Security Identity Theft   25
     Medical Identity Theft   31
     Character/ Criminal Identity Theft   37
     Financial Identity Theft   47

The Cost of being a victim   55

Going it ALONE   61

     Checklist   64
     Credit Freeze   69
     Fraud Alert   71

Identity Theft Report   77

     Activity Log   80
     Database Searches   81

Points of Contact   85

Victims Rights   95

Had Enough?   105

HOPE   107

Best Answer   115

Final Thoughts   119

Acknowledgements   123

Keeping the Lawyers Happy   125

Resources/ Statistics   127

About the Author

In a modern technological society where it's not a question of if your Identity will be stolen, but when, Mark Priganc is the one to trust. Mark is a graduate of Coastal Carolina University, with a Bachelor of Science in Business Management. Mark spent eight years with the United States Marine Corps. as a Combat Engineer, and whatever else the Marine Corps needed him to do. Mark is a combat veteran from Desert Storm. Given Mark's Marine Corps background, he is known for a tough, no nonsense approach with his clients, but when your future and good name are at stake, you need a reality check.

Mark Priganc is available for lectures and seminars in addition to his growing Identity Theft and information protection service plans. He has aligned himself with the best people in the industry to offer plans that will offer total protection for you, your family, and your business. He can be contacted at:

author@IdentityTheft-Reality.com

Dr. David W. Powers,
Founding Member of the U.S. Department of Homeland Security

What is Identity Theft?

"Identity Theft is the most insidious crime in America. It is a form of workplace violence, domestic abuse and terrorism. Identity Theft is an equal opportunity destroyer."

Supervisory Special Agent Robert G. Mitchell, FBI (retired) Visiting Professor in the Department of Justice, Law and Security. LaRoche College Pittsburgh, Pennsylvania

Identity Theft in simplest terms is: Any person, using your name, and/or personally identifying information, as his or her own without your permission. The Thief will use your information to commit fraud and other crimes. An Identity Thief will use your information in a traffic stop, to gain employment; to hide from law enforcement, to remain in the United States Illegally, the list goes on. The worst cases of Identity Theft are when the Thief becomes you.

In recent years, advances in computer technology have made it possible for detailed information about people to be compiled and shared very easily and less expensively than ever. This has produced many benefits for business, as well as the individual consumer. At the same time, as personal information has become more accessible, each of us - businesses, associations, government agencies, and consumers - must take precautions to protect against the misuse (also read as fraudulent use) of our personal information.

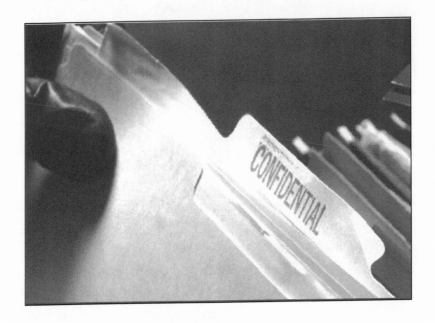

Identity Theft is a serious crime. While some Identity Theft victims can resolve their problems quickly, others spend hundreds or thousands of dollars and many days or months repairing damage to their good name and credit record. Some consumers victimized by Identity Theft may lose out on job opportunities, or denied loans for education, housing or cars because of negative information on their credit reports. In some cases, they may even be arrested for crimes they did not commit.

YOU WILL BE A VICTIM

"Information is the world's new currency,"
Secret Service Director W. Ralph Basham

If you are reading this book you will eventually be a victim of Identity Theft. Unfortunately you cannot predict when it will happen. But, you can prepare. Preparing means to educate yourself, and take proactive measures to reduce the impact on your life. The first step to proactive measures is in your hands now. You are educating yourself as to what Identity Theft really is. We'll get to other proactive measures later.

I hear you saying 'But, I shred everything. I don't buy anything online.' The list of 'I'm Careful' rationale is endless. You may not necessarily be the problem. The problem is your clone. Yea, that's right you have a clone. This clone has nothing to do with stem cell research or some dark scientific experiment. Your clone exists in the realm of 0's and 1's. That is how computers interpret the information that is fed into them. You see letters on this page that combine to form words. The computer sees these same words as combinations of 0's and 1's.
Your personal information is being fed into computers at many locations where you go everyday. The very fact that you were born has been entered into a computer.

Your personal information boils down to databases and companies called aggregators. These aggregators and databases compile information about you that they resell to various other companies.

News stories are breaking almost daily about data breaches. These breaches are everything from lost backup tapes, stolen laptops, and computer hardware to hacking, and physical thefts. Whatever the case your information is irretrievably out there.

Notable Examples:

> **Acxiom 1.6 BILLION** consumers information
CAUSE: HACKING
(This number represents approximately 1/3 of the world's   population)

> **Choicepoint 163,000** Provider of Background checks, drug screenings, Pre-Employment screenings. CAUSE: Bogus Accounts/ Customers

> **CardSystems: 40 Million** Cardholders. CAUSE: HACKING

> **Veterans Administration 28.6 Million** Veterans. CAUSE: Stolen Laptop

> **Ohio's Secretary of State (Cleveland, OH) 7.7 Million** Voters SSNs. CAUSE: CD-ROMs distributed to 20 political campaign operations.

> **AOL 92 Million Subscribers** CAUSE: Dishonest Employee. Sold entire database for $100,000.

Whatever the case your information is irretrievably out there.

Example:

Insurance companies buy consumer information for setting rates on health and life policies. Do you carry 'Preferred Shopper' key fobs? That information is sold to aggregators like Acxiom who in turn resell it to consumers of information (i.e. your insurance company). Did you tell the life insurance company that you are a non-smoker? Yet the grocery store 'Preferred Shopper' key fob shows that you buy two cartons of cigarettes every week. Now the life insurance company wants to talk to you about that fraudulent application.

In July 2003, a Russian computer hacker was sentenced in federal court to a prison term of four years for supervising a criminal enterprise in Russia dedicated to computer hacking, fraud, and extortion. The defendant hacked into the computer system of Financial Services, Inc. (FSI), an internet web hosting and electronic banking processing company located in Glen Rock, New Jersey, and stole 11 passwords used by FSI employees to access the FSI computer network as well as a text file containing approximately 3,500 credit card numbers and associated card holder information for FSI customers. One of the defendant's accomplices then threatened FSI that the hacker group would publicly release this stolen credit card information and hack into and further damage the FSI computer system unless FSI paid $6,000. After a period of negotiation, FSI eventually agreed to pay $5,000. In sentencing the defendant, the federal judge described the scheme as an unprecedented, wide-ranging, organized criminal enterprise that "engaged in numerous acts of fraud, extortion, and intentional damage to the property of others, involving the sophisticated manipulation of computer data, financial information, and credit card numbers." The court found that the defendant was responsible for an aggregate loss to his victims of approximately $25 million.

IDENTITY THEFT
Takes Many Forms

The federal government recognizes there are many forms of this crime, and thus has formed the Identity Theft Task Force. The FTC (Federal Trade Commission) has been tapped with spearheading the fight on Identity Theft, although there are numerous other federal agencies involved. The FTC tells us there are five different and very distinct, forms of Identity Theft. Thieves may use your information in any or all of these areas.

> **Drivers License Identity Theft**

> **Social Security Identity Theft**

> **Medical Identity Theft**

> **Character/ Criminal Identity Theft**

> **Financial Identity Theft**

Generally all you hear about is the Financial Identity Theft cases from the media. Well, that may be because the media is not fully aware of the depth of Identity Theft. I was interviewed recently for a newspaper article on Identity Theft; the reporter had no idea of the true scope of this crime. Granted, according to the FTC Financial Identity Theft comprise 28% of all reported cases they receive. That leads one to ask, what are the 72% of all other cases? Lets find out with a more in depth look at each area.

DRIVERS LICENSE
IDENTITY THEFT

Years ago using a fake ID to get into bars was the 'norm' especially around college campuses. Unfortunately the seemingly harmless 'fake ID' used to drink underage has morphed into a disturbing and sinister form of Identity Theft.

Computers and high-resolution printers along with a myriad of other technology hardware and software have made faking drivers licenses (DL's) and official ID cards all too easy. Let's say an Identity Thief gets hold of your DL information. Actually, take your license or ID card out and look at it... Now, imagine what your information would look like on another states license layout! You have no idea. Law enforcement personnel are not experts on what each states DL's look like either.

Many states used to and many still do sell DL information to whoever requests it. As long as the person requesting the information has an, 'Official' also read as 'Business' use for the information. Several states used to have your Social Security Number (SSN) listed as your DL number. As of this writing a couple of states still use your SSN. Thankfully that brilliant type of legislation is phasing out.

Whatever the case, your information is irretrievably out there.

This new 'Fake ID' contains your information with the thief's picture. The officer writes the ticket, the thief leaves the scene. That ticket goes unpaid. Subsequently a warrant can be issued for YOUR arrest, and your driving privileges can be suspended or revoked. Take this scenario from a simple ticket to a DUI/DWI charge. Now, the thief will have to pay the bail charge to get out of jail, but don't kid yourself into believing he/she will actually show up for the court date.

This is where you need to pay close attention! If you hold a professional license,

In an article entitled **"Waitress Gets Own ID When Carding Patron," the Associated Press reported that a bar waitress checking to see whether a patron was old enough to legally drink alcohol was handed her own stolen driver's license, which she reported missing weeks earlier in Lakewood, Ohio. The patron was later charged with identity theft and receiving stolen property.**

i.e. Medical, Stock Broker, Financial Planner, Insurance, Real Estate, Teaching, Child Care Provider, and so on. Your states professional licensing agency will take a VERY close look at you when a bench warrant is issued in your name. They may suspend, or worse, revoke your license to practice. The Identity Thief just stole your livelihood.

 So you don't hold a professional license. What do you think your car insurance company is going to do about that DUI/DWI issue? Or, the ticket you didn't know anything about?

Sure you can say 'But, it wasn't me' as the police handcuff you. Isn't that what every criminal says when the cold steel hits their wrists?

Identity Theft has flipped our judicial system 180 degrees. Instead, of innocent until proven guilty, you are guilty until you can prove yourself innocent. Law enforcements job is not to judicate who is or isn't guilty. They have a warrant in hand and must arrest the person whose information is on that warrant. In this case you have to prove yourself innocent because your personally identifying information has already been used in the commission of a crime.

Yes, you may eventually get the judicial system to listen to you. The question becomes how long will that take? And at what expense to you and your family: Physically, Mentally, and Financially?

That my dear reader is:
> Drivers License Identity Theft.

Stay with me…

There is **HOPE!**

Take a deep breath, calm down…

Social Security
Identity Theft

According to the FTC and Social Security Administration (SSA), best estimate is that there are 11 people using your Social Security Number (SSN) as you read this.

Employers must collect SSNs for tax reporting purposes. Doctors or hospitals may need them to facilitate Medicare reimbursement. SSNs also are used in internal systems to sort and track information about individuals, and in some cases are displayed on identification cards. In 2004, an estimated 42 million Medicare cards displayed the entire SSN, as did approximately 8 million Department of Defense insurance cards.

In June 2006, a federal judge in Massachusetts sentenced a defendant to five years in prison after a jury convicted him of passport fraud, SSN, fraud, aggravated Identity Theft, identification document fraud, and furnishing false information to the SSA. The defendant had assumed the Identity of a deceased individual and then used fraudulent documents to have the name of the deceased legally changed to a third name. He then used this new name and SSN to obtain a new SSN card, driver's licenses, and United States passport. The case was initiated based on information from the Joint Terrorism Task Force in Springfield Massachusetts. The agencies involved in the investigation included SSA OIG, Department of State, Massachusetts State Police, and the Springfield and Boston police departments.

SSNs are widely available in public records held by federal agencies, states, local jurisdictions, and courts. As of 2004, 41 states and the District of Columbia, as well as 75 percent of U.S. counties, displayed SSNs in public records. The number and type of records in which

SSNs are displayed varies greatly across states and counties, SSNs are most often found in court and property records.

In case you haven't noticed there is an Illegal immigration problem in this country. Yet, they all seem to be working various jobs. They must be using someone's SSN. That's right probably yours. In numerous parts of the country, illegal immigrants use fraudulently obtained SSNs or passports to obtain employment and assimilate into society. In many cases, an individual SSN may be passed on to and used by many illegal immigrants. Very few victims of this type of Identity Theft suffer financial harm. Those very few, must still spend hour upon hour attempting to correct their personal records to ensure that they are not mistaken for an illegal immigrant or cheated out of a government benefit. Unscrupulous employers knowingly accept non-valid SSNs. While others just don't know the numbers are invalid. Even the SSA takes their time researching a submitted SSN for verification.

The SSA knows your number is being used multiple times. They are not overly concerned about this. They need the money. The Federal Government has been using money from the SSA to fund pork barrel projects and expenses for a several decades (read as Republican and Democrat alike). Eleven people paying in for one number is seen as a cash cow for the SSA.

CLARIFICATION: Politicians see it this way. Therefore very little effort is given to curbing the illegal use of your SSN.

How is this, a problem for you?

Your SSN is the 'Holy Grail' of who you are, and what you can get: From Social Security Benefits, to financial aid for collage, Mortgages, car loans, medical benefits, and beyond.

This particular area of Identity Theft can tie into most of the other areas of Identity Theft as well.

First and foremost you need to know that your SSN is not correlated to your Race, Gender, Age, or even a picture of you.

With that said, now you understand why anyone can make use of your SSN.

Yet, the Social Security Administration remains nearly inactive to stemming the use of SSNs for accounts and IDing people.

They are slow to respond to verification requests from employers. The process can take upwards of a year to complete. By then the employer has paid into the system and withheld taxes, on your SSN.

They, the SSA, are not wholly responsible and individually responsible for this lack of concern. The

SSA answers to federal level politicians. Ponder that a few minutes.

When someone else uses your SSN to get set-up new financial accounts, those accounts may not show up on your Credit Reporting Agency (CRA) report. The CRA may simply place those new accounts into a sub-file. The sub-file will most likely be linked with your file, but you wont see the entire activity on your SSN. The reason is that Identity Thieves are so brazen that they will actually use their real name at times to further complicate the web of Identity Theft. It's not your name attached to those accounts, therefore you can't see the accounts.

Scenario:
An illegal immigrant uses your SSN to gain employment. They work their job. The employer withholds SS and tax monies from that worker. The worker does not file a tax return, for obvious reasons. The employer files their tax documents and reports that money was paid for your SSN. The IRS would like to talk with you about the failure on your part to report the income from your lettuce-picking job you earned in Arizona.

Federal Identity Theft charges were brought against 148 illegal aliens accused of stealing the identities of lawful U.S. citizens: in order to gain employment. The aliens being criminally prosecuted were identified as a result of Operation Wagon Train, an investigation led by agents from U.S. Immigration and Customs Enforcement (ICE), working in conjunction with six U.S. Attorney's Offices. Agents executed civil search warrants at six meat-processing plants. Numerous alien workers were arrested, and many were charged with aggravated Identity Theft, state Identity Theft, or forgery. Many of the names and Social Security numbers being used at the meat processing plants were reported stolen by Identity Theft victims to the FTC. In many cases, victims indicated that they received letters from the Internal Revenue Service demanding back taxes for income they had not reported because it was earned by someone working under their name. Other victims were denied driver's licenses, credit, or even medical services because someone had improperly used their personal information before.

These are just a couple of scenarios and examples of how thieves can and will use your SSN for fraud and leave you holding the bag of pooh.

Another deep breath…

Remember…

There is **HOPE**

Medical
Identity Theft

Medical Identity Theft is a crime in which the victim's identifying information is used to obtain or make false claims for medical care. In addition to the financial burdens associated with other types of Identity Theft,

victims of medical Identity Theft may have their health and life endangered by inaccurate entries in their medical records. Inaccurate information in your files can potentially cause victims to receive improper medical care, have your insurance depleted, become ineligible for health or life insurance, or become disqualified from some jobs. You as a victim may not even be aware that a theft has occurred because 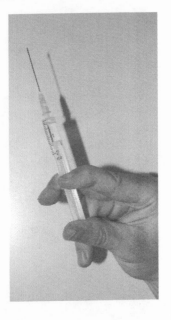 medical Identity Theft can be difficult to discover. Few consumers regularly review their medical records, and victims may not realize that they have been victimized until they receive collection notices, or they attempt to seek medical care themselves, only to discover that they have reached their coverage limits.

Thieves will use your information to gain or receive insurance benefits, Prescription Drugs, Medicare, Medicaid benefits, or for medical tests.

Did you know that you might have HIV, MS, Hepatitis, Diabetes, High Blood Pressure, or even Cancer?

What's in your File?

With the advent of the prescription drug benefit of Medicare Part D, the Department of Health and Human Services' Office of the Inspector General (HHS OIG) has noted a growing incidence of health care frauds involving Identity Theft. These frauds include telemarketers who fraudulently solicit potential Medicare Part D beneficiaries to disclose information such as their Health Insurance Claim Number (which includes the SSN) and bank account information, as well as marketers who obtain identities from nursing homes and other adult care facilities (including deceased beneficiaries and severely impaired persons) and use them fraudulently to enroll unwilling beneficiaries in alternate Part D plans in order to increase their sales commissions. The types of fraud that can be perpetrated by an Identity Thief are limited only by the ingenuity and resources of the criminal.

MIB: Yes there really is an MIB. Will Smith and Tommy Lee Jones don't star in this one. MIB stands for Medical Information Bureau. This is another aggregator of information. As their name implies they compile medical information. They compile the information that is presented to them, they have no means of verifying if the patient that was seen by doctors was actually you or not. The issues become more complex when you realize that the MIB is not the only aggregator of your medical information. Medical information has historically been a rather decentralized area. There are movements and legislation in progress that would centralize this information. The Pros to this centralization would be that it would be easier for you to verify the information that is actually in your file. It would be easier for random or annual check ups on your file. The Cons are, well, the exact same reasoning. Only, the thieves want the information  centralized so it is easier for them to get it all in one place. Kind of like the Wal-Mart®, get everything you need in a one-stop shopping trip.

In some cases the doctors themselves have been the thieves. The doctor agrees to help organized crime rings by inflating charges for services never rendered. Some doctor's offices will submit billing when the doctor never saw the patient. There are other instances when a worker in the office of the doctor will call in prescriptions for a 'patient' when in reality the office worker, picks up the prescription for themselves, either for personal use or to sell on the streets.

I hear you!

You're saying that you would simply call your doctor or the hospital and tell them that those charges are not yours. The situation isn't always that simple. There is a regulation called the Health Insurance Portability and Accountability Act (HIPAA). This regulation basically could keep you from seeing your own medical records if you were to tell the doctor or hospital that some charges, procedures, or surgeries are not yours.

Example:
This happened to a Colorado man. He received a bill from a hospital stating that he owed them over $40,000 for a surgical procedure, that he never had done. When he tried to correct the matter by going to the hospital. The staff refused to allow him to see 'his own records' because the signature on file and the signature on his Drivers License did not match.

Example:
A Florida woman received a bill from a local hospital asking her to pay for the amputation surgery she had done on one of her feet. After going back and forth with the hospital for several weeks she went to the hospital and put both of her feet up on the administrators desk to show both of her feet were hers and not prosthetics.

There are literally hundreds if not thousands of examples on the Internet describing horror stories of Medical Identity Theft, ranging for billing issues to misdiagnosing symptoms, and death. The tragic outcome is not always the doctor or hospitals fault. Identity Theft is literally killing people.

When was the last time you checked your medical file? Is what should be in there accurate? Are there diagnoses in there that shouldn't be there?

Keep in mind the HIPAA issues when addressing the items in your file. It would help you to consult with an attorney if there are errors in your file.

I'm sure you are catching on that Identity Theft is far more than someone stealing your credit cards and banking information.

Have you reached the point where you will never say: 'I wish someone would steal my Identity.'

Remember there is HOPE and we are getting closer to that hope. We just need to finish your introductory level education of Identity Theft first.

Deep Breath………….

Shake off the worries…

THERE IS **HOPE!**

CHARACTER/ CRIMINAL
IDENTITY THEFT

When the end of life comes your way, all you really will have is your good name.

Friends and business associates are in your life for three basic reasons:

> They Know You.

> They Like You.

> They Trust You.

Note: Family doesn't count in this instance. They are stuck with you, whether they like it or not.

When an Identity Thief begins using your name in the commission of crimes, your friends and business associates might begin to distance themselves from you.

Thieves literally become you in this area. They will live, work, and break the law using your name and personal information.

As you have already seen from above, organized crime uses Identity Theft to fund their activities. Law enforcement agencies around the country have noticed a steady increase in the involvement of groups and organizations of repeat offenders or career criminals in Identity Theft. Some of these groups—including nationwide gangs such as Hell's Angels, Neo-Nazis, and MS-13—are formally organized, having a 'chain of command' structure, and are well-known to law enforcement because of their longstanding involvement in other major crimes such as drug trafficking. Other groups are more loosely organized and, in some cases, have taken advantage of the Internet to organize, contact each other, and coordinate their Identity Theft activities more efficiently. Members of these groups often are located in different countries and communicate primarily via the Internet. Other groups have a real-world connection with one another and share a nationality or ethnic group. Law enforcement agencies also have seen increased involvement of foreign organized criminal groups in computer- or Internet-related Identity Theft schemes. In Asia and Eastern Europe, for example, organized groups are increasingly sophisticated both in the techniques they use to deceive Internet users into disclosing personal data, and in the complexity of tools they use, such as keyloggers (programs that record every keystroke as an Internet user logs onto his computer or a banking website), spyware (software that covertly gathers user information through the user's Internet connection, without the user's knowledge), and botnets (networks of computers that criminals have compromised and taken control of for some other purpose, ranging from distribution of spam and malicious computer code to attacks on other computers). According to law enforcement agencies, such groups also are demonstrating an increased level of sophistication and specialization in their online crimes, even selling goods and services—such as software templates for making counterfeit identification cards and payment card magnetic strip encoders—that make the stolen data even more valuable to those who have it.

Identity Theft is not a United States Phenomenon. Organized crime isn't Al Capone or Lucky Luciano. The images of what Hollywood has shown on the big screen for the last 50 plus years. Organized crime also means Terrorism. Terrorists use Identity Theft to move about more freely. Maybe that would explain the incident where an 8 year-old boy was banned from boarding a plane in Colorado. His name was on the Terrorist Watch List. Figure that one out!

Terrorists will use forged and counterfeit documents to gain access for travel, to the United States, and throughout the world.

The forged documents are such high quality that even the Department of Immigration, The State Department, and Customs missed the terrorists of the September 11th 2001 attacks.

Forged and counterfeit documents include passports and immigration forms.

© AarinFreePhoto.com

Example:

"A federal grand jury in Newark, New Jersey, alleges that the 19 individuals from across the United States and in <u>several foreign countries</u> conspired with others to operate "Shadowcrew," a website with approximately 4,000 members that was dedicated to facilitating malicious computer hacking and the dissemination of stolen credit card, debit card and bank account numbers and counterfeit identification documents, such as <u>drivers' licenses, passports and Social Security cards</u>. The indictment alleges a conspiracy to commit activity often referred to as "carding" - the use of account numbers and counterfeit Identity documents to complete Identity Theft and defraud banks and retailers." *United States DOJ*

OK, enough of the 'Big Picture' and the worldwide issues. Let's bring the thought of Identity Theft back down to the 'You' level.

Scenario:

Someone steals your wallet or purse. You take the 'appropriate steps' and file a police report, cancel your credit cards, change bank account information including your checking account, get a new Drivers License, etc. Are you secure now? Absolutely not! You may have stopped the thieves financially, for now. But, what stops that thief from starting an Internet site that caters to pornography, using your name and address for the registration information? The revenues can be sent to a bank account that they can open up with your information but their signature.

> "I was absolutely heartsick to realize our bank accounts were frozen, our names were on a bad check list, and my driver's license was suspended. I hold three licenses in the State of Ohio—my driver's license, my real estate license, and my R.N. license. After learning my driver's license was suspended, I was extremely fearful that my professional licenses might also be suspended as a result of the actions of my imposter."
>
> Maureen Mitchell
> Testimony Before
> House Committee on
> Financial Services,
> Subcommittee on
> Financial Institutions and
> Consumer Credit
> June 24, 2003

What kind of impact, will something like that scenario have on your life?

Are you a Teacher? A Child Care worker? A Pastor? A Police Officer? A Doctor? A Business Owner?

It doesn't matter what your livelihood is. That scenario can be devastating to your life and family.

A story like that hits your local news, and, the three reasons why you have friends and business associates will vanish.

People will not admit to knowing you. They wont be to keen on liking you. And, last but not least, they will not trust you.

That example is only the Character side of this area. What about the Criminal side?

We could simply use the same scenario from above and change the web site to a child pornography site. That will land you in jail!

'But, it wasn't me' as the police handcuff you. Isn't that what every criminal says when the cold steel hits their wrists?

That's scary stuff. Sure something like that may or may happen to you. So, let's ratchet down the 'worst case' a bit and take a look at a different scenario.

Scenario:

For space considerations, let's assume your wallet or purse, were stolen again. You have followed the same steps outlined above. This time the thief figures out that you have 'shut them down' financially, for now. The thief holds on to your information for a few months or even a year. In this time the thief relocates to another state. The thief now begins writing checks on the account that YOU closed. Obviously the checks will be returned because the account is closed. Your information is on the checks. YOU closed that account. YOU have some explaining to do.

That scenario is similar to what a man out of Tampa Fl. faced right before Christmas last year. He was arrested. Tampa police had an outstanding warrant from Texas for bad checks. This man was held for 58 days in a Tampa jail until the Department from Texas showed up to extradite him back to Texas. Fortunately, the man's family convinced an investigative reporter to look into the situation for them. The reporter discovered that a photo of the actual perpetrator was in the file in Texas. After repeated requests for that photo by the reporter, the Texas agency finally faxed it to them. The fax arrived the same day of the man's extradition. The reporter met the officers of both agencies at the airport, with the faxed picture in hand. The picture, which had been in the Texas police file the entire time, clearly showed that the man they wanted was not the man in custody. The man was released right there in the airport. He was given cab fare home and that was it. No apologies or anything else.

If you're sitting there reading through these scenarios having doubts as to the possibilities of this type of thing happening just Google® various search terms on Character and Criminal Identity Theft.

Recently a Milwaukee Wisconsin Police Officer admitted to being an illegal immigrant. He had assumed the Identity of his own dead cousin, in order to hide the fact that he was in the United States illegally. He subsequently used his cousin's name and other personal information to get his job as a Police Officer.

If you become a victim of Character or Criminal Identity Theft you could be arrested.

As of this writing, "Once your name is recorded in a criminal database, it's unlikely that it will be completely removed from the official record." *FTC publication 2006-332-381 pg. 21*
Even, if the information is proven to be inaccurate. You may, with the help of a good criminal attorney, be able to clear up <u>some</u> of this mess.

If you have indeed been arrested, you will need to carry an: 'official letter', 'clearance letter', or 'certificate of release' with you at all times. This official document will explain to the detaining officials, that you are not the individual actually being sought for those warrants.

It all comes down to this fact: Thieves will do whatever they can to hide, steal, and commit crimes. And, that 'whatever', means using your good name.

Deep Breath…………..

Shake off the visions of prison…

THERE IS **HOPE!**

FINANCIAL
IDENTITY THEFT

Here we are, the most thought of area involving Identity Theft, and now you know not the only area. As previously stated this area comprises 28% of all the complaints received by the FTC. The areas you just finished reading about are the other 72%.

Financial Identity Theft is probably the area that is most immediately felt by victims. Everyone, except those people living in a cave have, heard horror stories of financial Identity Theft. Google® this area and you will get tens of millions of hits.

Let's start with the "ZERO LIABILITY" Myth:

Zero Liability is in fact a myth. Here is why:

THE FAIR CREDIT BILLING ACT

"The Fair Credit Billing Act establishes procedures for resolving billing errors on your credit card accounts, including fraudulent charges on your accounts. The law also limits your liability for unauthorized credit card charges to $50 per card. To take advantage of the law's consumer protections, you **MUST**:

> ➤ Write to the creditor at the address given for 'billing inquiries' NOT the address for sending your payments. Include you name, address, account number, and a description of the billing error, including the amount and date of the error.
> ➤ Send your letter so that it reaches the creditor within 60 days after the first bill containing the

error was mailed to you. **If an Identity thief changes the address on your account and you didn't receive the bill, your dispute letter still must reach the creditor within 60 days of when the creditor would have mailed the bill**... or will you owe the money.
FTC publication 2006-332-381

Your ATM and Debit Card:

The Electronic Fund Transfer Act provides consumer protections for transactions involving their ATM or debit card, or another electronic way to debit or credit an account. This act also limits your liability for unauthorized electronic fund transfers.

Here again as with your Credit Cards: You have 60 days from the date your bank account statement is sent to you to report in writing any money withdrawn from your account without your permission. This includes instances when your ATM or debit card is "skimmed" that is, when a thief captures your account number and PIN without your card having been lost or stolen.

Example:

"Waiters in about 40 restaurants, in New York and elsewhere, covertly recorded customers' credit card information and passed it on to people who used the information to make more than $3 million worth of illegal purchases, according to court documents. The district attorney said, in the complaint that, conspiracy leaders recruited and managed people who worked as waiters and provided them with small, **hand-held "skimmers"** that read and recorded information contained on the magnetic strips of patrons' credit cards. The leaders, some of whom worked in the restaurants with their recruits, then collected the **skimming devices,** and then paid the waiters **$35 to $50 for information from each credit card stored in the devices"** *FOIA, Police Reports/Court documents*

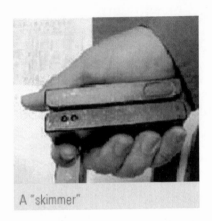

A "skimmer"

A variation of skimming involves an ATM-mounted device that is able to capture the magnetic information on the consumer's card, as well as the consumer's password.

If your ATM or debit card is lost or stolen, report it immediately because the amount you can be held responsible for depends on **how quickly** you report the loss.

- ➤ If you report the loss or theft within **two business days** of discovery, your losses are limited to $50.
- ➤ If you report the loss or theft after two business days, but within 60 days after the unauthorized electronic fund transfer appears on your statement, **you could lose up to $500 of what the thief withdraws.**

> If you wait **more than 60 days** to report the loss or theft, **you could lose all the money that was taken from your account** after the end of the 60 days.

Note: VISA and MasterCard voluntarily have agreed to limit consumers' liability for unauthorized use of their debit cards in most instances to $50 per card, no matter how much time has elapsed since the discovery of the loss or theft of the card.

The best way to protect yourself in the event of an error or fraudulent transaction is to call the financial institution and follow up in writing by certified letter, return receipt requested so you can prove when the institution received your letter. Keep a copy of the letter you send for your records.

Examples of Timeliness:

Bank of America® has filed suit against a Bronx NY woman for overdraft charges. This woman had filed a police report and fraud report. The bank was slow to respond to her complaints and reports. Several events transpired in this woman's life, time went by. To the ladies dismay she found a court subpoena at her home, notifying her of the lawsuit being brought by Bank of America®'

You would think that your own financial institution would go to bat for you. Obviously with this story, you need to rethink who is really on your side when you become the victim.

'Homecomings Financial Network Inc.® (A subsidiary of GMAC® Financial Services) sued a family for $75,000, plus attorney's fees. This family had once held a home equity line of credit with Homecomings. While attempting to refinance their current home, they found $75,000 of unauthorized charges on the old equity line, contained in their credit report. An Identity Thief had changed the address for that line of credit and the family never knew the charges had occurred. The family thought they had straightened it out, especially since they had paperwork in hand absolving them of the debt. Homecomings, after two years, decided to sue them. Homecomings' reasoning is that this family was slow to discover the fraud. Homecomings subsequently dropped the suit but without prejudice. In other words, Homecomings reserved their right to go after them again. *FOIA*

If an Identity Thief targets you, one of the first things they will do is change your address. Have you noticed how convenient (also read as easy) it is to change an address these days? It is so easy to change, an address, you can even do this online, in your underwear (or your preferred lounging attire). Given what you have just read about the requirements concerning billing errors you need to ask yourself a question: "What do I do about those pre-approved card offers that are floating around out there?" You know- the ones an Identity Thief has gotten for you. But, the card and bill goes to some other address. Remember you only have 60 days to dispute those charges. Otherwise, YOU are responsible.

Let's go PHISHING!

No, that's not a typo. That is the new millennium way to spell an ageless activity. Phishing is a method used by spammers (Identity Thieves) on the Internet. They cast millions of lines (emails) into the water of the Internet. Approximately 5% of those people that receive these Phishing lines nibble on the bait. The preferred bait by these spammers is generally a ruse from a financial institution or brokerage house. They claim to be upgrading their web-based security measures. They need you to enter your account information to complete the 'process'. Memorize this next item:

DON'T EVER RESPOND TO THESE CRIMINALS!!!!

You may think to yourself "I'll just call the number in the email to see if it is really for my bank." The spammers have thought the same thing. Therefore they have put a real number to your bank in the email so when you call it, you will get your bank on the line. Don't even think about it! See above! Financial institutions will not ask you for your personal information over the Internet. If you absolutely must think this Phishing scam is real go into your bank personally. They can set you straight in a face-to-face meeting. Phishing recently has taken on a new form, dubbed "Vishing," in which the thieves use Voice

Over Internet Protocol (VOIP) technology to spoof the telephone call systems of financial institutions and request callers provide their account information.
Up until now you probably thought that financial Identity Theft was the only area you needed to concern yourself with. I can understand that train of thought. Most people fear a financial loss more than anything else when it comes to Identity Theft.

Now you know.

This is a far-reaching crime with major issues in play. Your eyes are opening to what it is.

There is…

HOPE

THE COST
OF BEING A VICTIM

The full gamut of Identity Theft is still evolving. Every-time law enforcement comes up with a new method of attack on the perpetrators they change their MO. The methods become more difficult to track. The 'swap-rooms' become harder to find (for law enforcement). It will be a never-ending chase to catch the thieves.

Once your information is in the hands of the thieves they can sell it over and over again. Each time they sell it they can get anywhere from $25 for a DL to $200 or more for medical insurance. Each time they resell your information they create more trouble for you. That trouble comes in the form of multi-jurisdictional crimes.

Now we are getting into the area where you really need to take heed.

Here is another item for you to <u>never forget</u>:

Amateurs will use your information locally. Professionals will use your information outside of your local area.

Truth be-known, only 1 in 700 Identity Thieves are ever prosecuted. Other than the fact that they are elusive, and digital, what would you imagine an Identity Thief to look like?
Unlike some groups of criminals, Identity Thieves cannot be readily recognized. Virtually no statistics have been compiled to provide comprehensive information on their personal or demographic

characteristics. For the most part, victims are not in a good position to know who stole their information or who misused it. According to the FTC's 2003 survey of Identity Theft, only about 14 percent of victims claim to know the perpetrator.

According to law enforcement agencies, Identity thieves often have no prior criminal background and sometimes have pre-existing relationships with the victims. Indeed, Identity Thieves have been known to prey on people they know, including coworkers, senior citizens for whom they are serving as caretakers, and even their own family members. Some Identity Thieves rely on methods of minimal sophistication, such as stealing mail from homeowners' mailboxes or trash containing financial documents. In some jurisdictions, Identity Theft by illegal immigrants has resulted in passport, employment, and Social Security fraud. Occasionally, small clusters of individuals with no significant criminal records work together in a loosely knit fashion to obtain personal information and even to create false and/or fraudulent documents. A number of recent reports have focused on the connection between individual methamphetamine ("meth") users and Identity Theft. Law enforcement agencies in Albuquerque, Honolulu, Phoenix, Sacramento, Seattle, and other cities have reported that meth addicts are engaging in Identity and data theft through burglaries, mail theft, and theft of wallets and purses. In Salt Lake City, meth users reportedly are organized by white-supremacist gangs to commit Identity Theft. Tellingly, as meth use has risen sharply in recent years, especially in the western United States, some of the same jurisdictions reporting the highest levels of meth use also suffer from the highest incidence of Identity Theft. Some state law enforcement officials believe that the two increases might be related, and that Identity Theft may serve as a major funding mechanism for meth labs and purchases.

An Identity Thief could be your next-door neighbor, the lady behind the counter at your favorite coffee shop, waiters, or the cleaning crew at your bank. The list of possible thieves is endless, yet faceless. Their victims are all but faceless. Their crimes are all but victimless. And each poses unique threats to the public.

The FTC tells us that losses are in the $53 billion range annually. They are compiling figures reported by various businesses. What aren't included in their figures are the losses on a personal level. How do you quantify the anxiety, the stress, and the physical strain on a victim of this crime? That is the real cost of this crime not the dollars and cents figures I am about to show you.

> The average dollar amount charged in Identity Theft: **$92,893**

> The average number of checks written in Identity Theft: **74.6**

> The average number of credit card applications approved through Identity Theft: **8.4**

These figures don't include the legal expenses you could be facing in the wake of an Identity Theft incident in your life. Legal expenses alone could cost you in the realm of $20,000. Even the FTC is upfront enough with you to tell you that you are going to need legal council. Remember the point from above:

Amateurs will use your information locally. Professionals will use your information outside of your local area.

Given that professionals are more apt to get hold of your information. They will be crossing county lines, even state lines. You are going to need lawyers in many states not just your local area. Lawyers need to be licensed in a state where they desire to practice. To be more specific, you need an attorney that knows their way around the web of Identity Theft.

Now that you are almost finished with your Identity Theft education at the beginner level, you can appreciate the full spectrum of this crime.
This brings us to…

Going it ALONE

As you already read above, it can take you upwards of 600 hours to restore your Identity on your own. To show that I am not only writing this book to sell you my services, below are actions and resources that can get you on your way to restoring your good name. If you insist on going it ALONE, all I can say is Good Luck!

The easiest way for me to explain how you can take your own proactive actions toward protecting your Identity is to have you visualize yourself as a tightrope walker.

Your hands are stretched out to the sides. In one hand you hold the security that you desire for your Identity. In the other hand you hold the convenience of modern lifestyle: rapid check-outs, saved passwords on your favorite websites, online shopping, ATMs, Debit Cards, Touch-N-Go®, Fingerprint pay, credit cards at the restaurant, the list goes on and on.

You have to find that balance point for your own life as to how much security you desire and how much convenience you would like to have. If you want every modern convenience available in the marketplace, you are sure to fall prey to the Identity Thieves. I'm not saying avoid all of the modern conveniences. I am simply saying find your balance point. You may tend to feel annoyed when the cashier at your favorite store asks to see picture ID. Don't be, that store is helping you with your **Conscurity**™ (The balance of convenience and security). You may have to give up some of those convenient ways of life, while at the same time giving up some of those anal security measures. You can find **Conscurity**™ in your life. It will take some effort. But aren't you worth the effort?

Lets look at some steps on the tightrope that you can take to achieve **Conscurity**™. Please note that these are examples of what you can do on your own to attempt to mitigate the damage an Identity Thief can do to your good name (Professional assistance may be a necessity). Be aware of what may or may not apply to your specific state. Some state specific listings are available at: www.IdentityTheft-Reality.com

Every day we share personal information about ourselves with others. It's so routine that you may not even realize you're doing it. You write a check at the grocery store, charge tickets to a ball game, rent a car, mail your tax returns, buy a gift online, call home on your cell phone, schedule a doctor's appointment or apply for a credit card. Each of those transactions require that you share personal information: your bank and credit card account numbers; your income; your Social Security number (SSN); or your name, address and phone numbers.

It's important to find out what happens to the personal information you provide to companies, marketers and government agencies. These organizations may use your information simply to process your order; to tell you about products, services, or promotions; or <u>to share with others</u>.

CHECKLIST

➢ Before you reveal any personally identifying information, find out how it will be used and whether it will be shared with others. Ask about a company's Information Security Policy: Will you have a choice about the use of your information; can you choose to have it kept confidential?

➢ Read the privacy policy on any website directed to children. Websites directed to children or that knowingly collect information from kids under 13 must post a notice of their information collection practices.

➢ Put passwords on your all your accounts, including your credit card account, and your bank and phone accounts.

➢ Minimize the identification information and the number of cards you carry to what you'll actually need. Don't put all your identifying information in one holder in your purse, briefcase or backpack.

➢ Keep items with personal information in a safe place. When you discard receipts, copies of credit applications, insurance forms, physician statements, bank checks and statements, expired charge cards, credit offers you get in the mail and mailing labels from magazines, tear or shred (Cross-Cut or Diamond-Cut) them. That will help deter any Identity Thief who may pick through your trash or recycling bins to capture your personal information.

➢ Order a copy of your credit report from each of the three major credit-reporting agencies (CRAs) every year. A good method for keeping up on your reports is to order a report from one agency every quarter throughout the year. Make sure it's accurate and includes only those activities you've authorized. CRAs cannot charge you more than $9.00 for a copy and in some states; your credit report is free.

➢ Use a secure browser when shopping online to guard the security of your transactions. When submitting your purchase information, look for the "lock" icon on the browser's status bar, generally in the lower right corner, to be sure your information is secure during transmission.

➢ Purchase a lockable mailbox for your home. The postal carrier can slide your mail through a slot in the front. Many cases of Identity Theft occur from stolen mail.

➢ Use a United States Postal Mailbox or the Post Office for outgoing mail.

➢ Opt-Out of pre-screened credit card offers. Go to www.IdentityTheft-Reality.com for the forms to do this.

➢ If you have not been opting-out of the information sharing 'Privacy Policy' for your credit cards, cell phone provider, doctor, insurances, or banks. You need to do so now! Go to www.IdentityTheft-Reality.com for the Revocation Letter. Send or give this letter to all of the people you do business with that collect personal information on you.

➢ When using your Debit card for a purchase, cover the keypad as you enter your PIN number. Better yet, have the cashier run your debit card as a credit card, then, you don't have to enter your PIN.

➢ DO NOT carry your Social Security card in your purse or wallet.

➢ If your Drivers License is lost or stolen, demand a new DL number when you get it replaced. It may be inconvenient to learn a new number, but it would be even more inconvenient to be arrested for something you didn't do. Remember the cold steel on your wrists!

➢ Only put a first initial with your last name on your checks. Not your full name. Thieves wont know your gender and thus have a more difficult time using your checks.

➢ If your bank will allow it, put 'Check Picture ID' in place of your address. This will place the address verification responsibility on the store. This will prove they checked the ID of the person writing the check. This makes using your checks more of an annoyance to thieves.

➢ Make sure no one is looking over your shoulder at ATMs, pay phones, or the Debit Card Keypad.

➢ Shield your credit cards from view when making purchases. Thieves can use a camera phone to take a picture of your card.

➢ Use 'STRONG' passwords for everything that requires one. A 'STRONG' password is one that contains a combination of letters and numbers, upper case and lower case letters. Your birthday with the month spelled out and numbers for the day and year IS NOT a 'STRONG' password.

This checklist is a mere sample of everything you can do on your own. It comes down to using common sense. Think before you divulge private information.

THINK:
> Who is Asking?
> What are they Asking?
> Why are they Asking?
> Why do They Need that Information?
> What is their Information Security Policy?
> Will you have the Opportunity to Opt-Out?
> Who is Listening?
> Who is Watching?

You get the idea right?

Credit Freeze

What is a credit freeze?

Many states- not all- have laws that let consumers restrict access to their credit report. If you place a credit freeze, potential creditors and other third parties will not be able to get access to your credit report unless you temporarily lift the freeze. This means that it's unlikely that an Identity thief would be able to open a new account in your name. Placing a credit freeze does not affect your credit score – nor does it keep you from getting your free annual credit report, or from buying your credit report or score.

> *Note: You are entitled to one free report from each credit-reporting agency per year. If you wish to obtain additional reports within that year you can do so at a cost of $9.00, in some states additional reports are free as well.*

Credit freeze laws vary from state to state. In some states, anyone can freeze their credit file, while in other states, only Identity Theft victims can. The cost of placing, temporarily lifting, and removing a credit freeze also varies. There is a cost involved with each action. Many states make credit freezes free for

Identity Theft victims, while other consumers pay a fee – typically $10 for each action. It's also important to know that these costs are for <u>each</u> of the credit reporting agencies. If you want to freeze your credit, it would mean placing the freeze with each of three credit-reporting agencies, and paying the fee to each one. Refer to the back of this book for a listing, of states credit freeze laws. You may also go to:

www.IdentityTheft-Reality.com

Fraud Alert

What is a fraud alert?
There are two types of fraud alerts: an **initial** alert, and an **extended** alert.

➢ **An initial fraud alert stays on your credit report for at least 90 days.** You may ask that an initial fraud alert be placed on your credit report if you suspect you have been, or are about to be, a victim of Identity Theft. An initial alert is appropriate if your wallet has been stolen or if you've been taken in by a "Phishing" or "Vishing" scam. With an initial fraud alert, potential creditors must use what the law refers to as "reasonable policies and procedures" to verify your identity before issuing credit in your name. However, the steps potential creditors take to verify your identity may not always alert them that the applicant is not you. When you place an initial fraud alert on your credit report, you're entitled to order one free credit report from each of the three nationwide consumer reporting companies, and, if you ask, only the last four digits of your Social Security number will appear on your credit reports.

> **An extended fraud alert stays on your credit report for seven years.** You can have an extended alert placed on your credit report if you've been a victim of identity theft and you provide the consumer reporting company with an <u>Identity Theft Report</u>. With an extended fraud alert, potential creditors must actually contact you, or meet with you in person, before they issue you credit. When you place an extended alert on your credit report, you're entitled to two free credit reports within twelve months from each of the three nationwide consumer reporting companies. In addition, the consumer reporting companies will remove your name from marketing lists for pre-screened credit offers for five years unless you ask them to put your name back on the list before then.

To place either of these alerts on your credit report, or to have them removed, you will be required to provide appropriate proof of your identity: that may include your Social Security number, name, address and other personal information requested by the consumer reporting company.

As mentioned, depending on the type of fraud alert you place, potential creditors must either contact you or take reasonable steps to verify your Identity. This may cause some delays if you're trying to obtain credit. To compensate for possible delays, you may want to include a cell phone number, where you can be reached easily, in your alert. Remember to keep all contact information in your alert current.

What doesn't a fraud alert do?

A fraud alert can help keep an Identity Thief from opening new accounts in your name. It's not a solution to <u>all types</u> of Identity Theft. It will not protect you from an Identity Thief using your existing credit cards or other accounts. It also will not protect you from an Identity Thief opening new accounts in your name that do not require a  credit check – such as a telephone, wireless, or bank account. It won't necessarily help you in the DL, Medical, or SSN Identity Theft areas. And, if there's Identity Theft already going on when you place the fraud alert, the fraud alert alone won't stop it. A fraud alert, however, can be useful in stopping Identity Theft that involves opening a new line of credit.

The differences between a credit freeze and a fraud alert

A fraud alert is tool for people who have had their Identity stolen – or who suspect it may have been stolen. With a fraud alert in place, businesses may still check your credit report. Depending on whether you place an initial 90-day fraud alert or an extended fraud alert, potential creditors must either contact you or use what the law refers to as "Reasonable Policies and Procedures" to verify your Identity before issuing credit in your name. However, the steps potential creditors take to verify your Identity may not always alert them that the applicant is not you.

A credit freeze, on the other hand, will prevent potential creditors and other third parties from accessing your credit report at all, unless you lift the freeze or already have a relationship with the company. Some consumers use credit freezes because they feel they give more protection. As with credit freezes, fraud alerts are mainly effective against new credit accounts being opened in your name, but will likely not stop thieves from using your existing accounts, or opening new accounts such as new telephone or wireless accounts,

> **The FTC receives about 15,000 to 20,000 contacts each week on how to recover from identity theft or how to avoid becoming a victim in the first place. The Federal Trade Commission has distributed over 1.5 million brochures and 40,000 kits to date"**
> *FTC Chairman Deborah Platt Majors*

where credit is often not checked. Also, only people who've had their ID stolen – or who suspect it may have been stolen, may place fraud alerts. In some states, anyone can place a credit freeze.

Keep in mind, financial institutions are required to take 'Reasonable Measures' to verify the Identity of the person seeking credit or a new account.

'Reasonable Measures' is not a clearly defined term in the laws I have seen pertaining to Identity Theft. Your idea of Reasonable may not match a lending institutions definition of Reasonable. Ask to review their 'Information Security Policy' and Privacy Policy.

Creating an Identity Theft Report

An Identity Theft Report can be used to permanently block fraudulent information from appearing on your credit report. An Identity Theft Report will also make sure these debts do not reappear on your credit report. An Identity Theft Report can prevent a company from continuing to collect debts that result from Identity Theft, or selling them to others for collection. An Identity Theft Report is also <u>required,</u> to place, an extended fraud alert on your credit report.

Creating an Identity Theft Report will require two steps or actions on your part:

FIRST STEP: Obtain a copy of a report filed with a local, state, or a federal law enforcement agency, like your local police department, your State Attorney General, the FBI, the U.S. Secret Service, the FTC, or the U.S. Postal Inspection Service. There are no federal laws requiring a federal agency to take a report about Identity Theft; however, some state laws require local police departments to take reports. The law requires the report to provide as much information as you can about the crime, including anything you know about the dates of the Identity Theft, the fraudulent accounts opened and the alleged Identity Thief. If you do not provide detailed information, it may be impossible for consumer reporting companies and creditors to comply with your requests. I suggest that you file an online Complaint form with the FTC, and then ask your local police department to incorporate a copy of the printed Identity Theft Complaint into the police report. By following this procedure, the consumer reporting company and the information provider may require less additional information and/or documentation under Step Two.

SECOND STEP: This depends on the policies of the consumer reporting company and the information provider (the business that sent the information to the consumer reporting company). That is, they may ask you to provide information or documentation in addition to that included in the law enforcement report, which is reasonably intended to verify your Identity Theft. They must make their request within 15 days of receiving your law enforcement report, or, if you already obtained an extended fraud alert on your credit report, the date you submit your request to the credit reporting company for information blocking. The consumer reporting company and information provider then have 15 more days to work with you to make sure your Identity Theft Report contains everything they need. They are entitled to take five days to review any information you give them. For example, if you give them information 11 days after they request it, they do not have to make a final decision until 16 days after they asked you for that information. If you give them any information after the 15-day deadline, they can reject your Identity Theft Report as incomplete; you will have to resubmit your Identity Theft Report with the correct information.

You may find that most federal and state agencies, and some local police departments, offer only "automated" reports, reports that do not require a face-to-face meeting with a law enforcement officer. Automated reports may be submitted online, or by telephone or mail. If you have a choice, do not use an automated report. The reason? It's more difficult for the consumer reporting company or information provider to verify the information. Unless you are asking a consumer reporting company to place an extended fraud alert on your credit report, if you use an automated report the consumer reporting company or information provider will probably ask you to provide additional information or documentation.

Now let's begin to really get our hands dirty with this mess!

Creating an Activity Log

Once you realize the Identity Theft Reaper has come your way, log/ write down EVERYTHING you do. Maintain file folders for each credit and debit card that you have. In these file folders keep your receipts. Reconcile (match your receipts with the charges posted by your creditor) all of these accounts every month when your statements come in. Note on a calendar when each statement comes in from your creditor. This is important to know, so if an Identity Thief steals your statement, you can contact your creditor. Remember Thieves will also change your address on your statements. Most credit card companies make this step easier for you by allowing you to set your payment as well as your statement date. Remember to include your investment accounts as well.

Track every phone call you make relating to your Identity Theft. Write down:

- ➤ Who you spoke with.
- ➤ The Company or Agency they work for.
- ➤ When you spoke with them: Time and Date.
- ➤ The time Length of the call or conversation.
- ➤ Synopsis of the call or conversation (i.e. TAKE NOTES!)
    - o *If you are face-to-face, have the other person or persons sign-off on your notes that you have taken during the meeting.*

- ➤ What your next action step is with that Company or Agency.

You can find a printable form for your use at: www.IdentityTheft-Reality.com

Databases Searches

Your next task when 'Going it ALONE' and creating your Identity Theft Report is to begin your database searches. There are numerous companies that provide your criminal background, birth dates, current and previous addresses, bankruptcy filings, sex offender check, alias names, home value and details, and the likes. Most of these searches will be for a single state. The fees for these searches range from free to over $100. The free stuff is basically phonebook searches. An average cost will be in the $45 range per state ($2,250 approx. cost for all 50 states). The price is determined by how much information you want to find.

The next task with the databases will be to begin searching all of the property databases, court records (traffic, criminal, probate, family, bankruptcy, and civil), tax, and aggregators, throughout the United States. Each county maintains their-own databases. The Census Bureau lists 3,141 counties in the United States. There are few cities that maintain their own records within a county. Add those to your list of searches.

After you finish with the property databases, and court records, turn your focus toward the medical industry. This would include hospitals, doctor's offices, and clinics. This could prove to be a near impossibility. To begin and possibly narrow your search, start with the MIB. You do have a right to review what is in your MIB file.

Note: If you are planning on changing your medical coverage, the MIB route could be a two-edged sword. Meaning, by pulling this report could possibly send up red flags to potential insurers. They will invariably want to know more about you before issuing a policy.

If you are the ambitious type, start with the hospitals. There are 7,569 hospitals in the United States. Or, you could focus on dealing with the doctors and doctor offices; there are 819,000 of them. Be aware that these numbers do not include the clinics, or Doc-In-The-Box establishments.

Listed below is a list of contacts. You can start with it. Or, I think you may be getting the idea that going it alone may not be such a wise idea. Although, I run into people everyday that would rather try and save $13 to $36 per month and go through what has just been described to you. These very same people would rather pay $100 per month for cable television than to be smart enough to invest in something that could protect their family.

Enough soapbox preaching, you're the choir. Let's move on.

Points of Contact

CREDIT BUREAUS

EQUIFAX—http://www.equifax.com/
To order your credit report:
Call: (800) 685-1111
Write: Equifax
P.O. Box 740241
Atlanta, GA 30374-0241

To report fraud:
Call: (800) 525-6285
Write: Equifax
Fraud Assistance
P.O. Box 105069
Atlanta, GA 30348

EXPERIAN—http://www.experian.com/
To order your credit report:
Call: (888) EXPERIAN (397-3742)
Write: Experian
P.O. Box 2104
Allen, TX 75013-2104
To report fraud:
Call: (888) EXPERIAN (397-3742)
Write: Experian
P.O. Box 9530
Allen, TX 75013

TRANS UNION—http://www.tuc.com/
To order your credit report:
Call: (800) 916-8800
Write: Trans Union
P.O. Box 34012
Fullerton, CA 92834

To report fraud:
Call: (800) 680-7289
Write: Trans Union
Fraud Victim Assistance Department
P.O. Box 6790
Fullerton, CA 92834-6790

HOW YOU CAN . . .

REMOVE YOUR NAME FROM PRE-APPROVED CREDIT LISTS:

Call: (888) 5OPTOUT (888-567-8688)
This, removes your name from pre-approved credit lists compiled by Equifax, Experian, and Trans Union.

REMOVE YOUR NAME FROM DIRECT MAIL LISTS:

Internet: http://www.the-dma.org/
Write: Direct Marketing Association
Mail Preference Service
P.O. Box 643
Carmel, NY 10512

REMOVE YOUR NAME FROM TELEPHONE LISTS:

Internet: http://www.the-dma.org/
Write: Direct Marketing Association
Telephone Preference Service
P.O. Box 1559
Carmel, NY 10512

REMOVE YOUR NAME FROM E-MAIL LISTS:

Internet: http://www.e-mps.org/

REPORT STOLEN OR FRAUDULENT USE OF YOUR CHECKS OR CREDIT CARDS:

Contact your bank or credit card issuer and close your bank account or credit card account immediately.

MORE INFORMATION ON IDENTITY THEFT
FEDERAL LEVEL:

FEDERAL BUREAU OF INVESTIGATION (FBI)

http://www.fbi.gov/

The FBI investigates federal Identity Theft cases, including those where an Identity thief used your personal identifying information to commit a crime. Although the FBI generally investigates cases where there is a significant dollar loss (i.e. over $200,000), your information may provide evidence of a larger pattern of fraud. If your Identity has been stolen, call your local FBI field office. Local FBI field offices are listed in the Government section of your White Pages telephone directory.

FEDERAL TRADE COMMISSION (FTC)

http://www.consumer.gov/idtheft

The FTC has a hotline for Identity Theft victims and provides victims with information to help resolve financial and other problems resulting from Identity Theft. If your Identity has been stolen, contact the FTC at the Identity Theft Hotline listed below or call your local FTC field office. Local FTC field offices are listed in the Government section of your White Pages telephone directory.

Call: (877) IDTHEFT (877-438-4338)
TDD: (202) 326-2502
Write: Identity Theft Clearinghouse
Federal Trade Commission
600 Pennsylvania Ave., N.W.
Washington, DC 20580

INTERNAL REVENUE SERVICE (IRS)

http://www.treas.gov/irs/ci

The IRS administers and enforces federal tax laws. If someone has filed fraudulent federal tax returns or committed other tax fraud in your name, contact the IRS at the Criminal Investigation Informant Hotline listed below or call your local IRS field office. Local IRS field offices are listed in the Government section of your White Pages telephone directory.
Call: (800) 829-0433

SOCIAL SECURITY ADMINISTRATION/ OFFICE OF INSPECTOR GENERAL (SSA/OIG)

http://www.ssa.gov/oig

The SSA/OIG investigates Identity Theft cases involving the fraudulent use of social security numbers. If someone has stolen your social security card or fraudulently used your social security number, contact the SSA/OIG at the telephone number listed below or call your local SSA/OIG field office. Local SSA/OIG field offices are listed in the Government section of your White Pages telephone directory.

Call: (800) 269-0271
Write: Social Security Fraud Hotline
P.O. Box 17768
Baltimore, MD 21235

UNITED STATES DEPARTMENT OF JUSTICE (DOJ)
http://www.usdoj.gov/criminal/fraud/idtheft.html

UNITED STATES ATTORNEY'S OFFICE (USAO)

The DOJ and its USAOs prosecute federal Identity Theft crimes. The website listed above contains information on Identity Theft.

UNITED STATES TRUSTEE'S OFFICE (USTO)

http://www.usdoj.gov/ust

The DOJ and its USTOs oversee all bankruptcy filings. If someone has fraudulently filed a bankruptcy case in your name, or fraudulently used your social security number in a bankruptcy filing, contact the USTO in the region where the bankruptcy case was filed. USTOs are listed in the Government section of your White Pages telephone directory.

UNITED STATES DEPARTMENT OF STATE/ DIPLOMATIC SECURITY SERVICE (USDOS/DSS)

http://www.travel.state.gov/passport_services.html

The USDOS/DSS is responsible for issuing passports. If someone has stolen or fraudulently used your passport, contact the USDOS/DSS at the website listed above or call your local USDOS/DSS field office. Local USDOS/DSS field offices are listed in the Government section of your White Pages telephone directory.

UNITED STATES POSTAL INSPECTION SERVICE (USPIS)

http://www.usps.gov/websites/depart/inspect

The USPIS investigates Identity Theft cases involving the U.S. mail. If your mail has been stolen, someone has fraudulently changed the mailing address on your bank or credit card accounts, or someone has used the

mail as part of an Identity Theft scheme, contact the USPIS. Locate the nearest USPIS district office through the website listed above or by calling the telephone number listed below.
Call: (800) 275-8777

UNITED STATES SECRET SERVICE (USSS)

http://www.treas.gov/usss

The USSS investigates federal financial crimes, including those involving Identity Theft. Although the USSS generally investigates cases where there is a significant dollar loss, your information may provide evidence of a larger pattern of fraud. If a financial crime has been committed in your name, contact the USSS at the website listed above or call your local USSS field office. Local USSS field offices are listed in the Government section of your White Pages telephone directory.

UNITED STATES SECURITIES AND EXCHANGE COMMISSION (SEC)

http://www.sec.gov/

The SEC handles complaints about investment fraud and the mishandling of investments by securities professionals. If someone has misused your Identity in connection with a securities transaction, contact the SEC at the telephone number listed below or call your local SEC field office. Local SEC field offices are listed in the Government section of your White Pages telephone directory.

Call: (202) 942-7040
Write: Securities and Exchange Commission, 450 Fifth Street, N.W., Washington, DC 20549-0213

Identity Theft Victim's Rights

Several federal laws protect victims of Identity Theft. These laws have to do with documenting the theft; dealing with credit reporting companies; dealing with creditors, debt collectors, and merchants; and limiting your financial losses caused by the theft of your Identity. Here is a brief summary of the rights of Identity Theft victims.

Documenting the Theft

You have the right to:

> ➢ File a report with a law enforcement agency and ask for a copy of it to show how your Identity has been misused. This report is often called a police report.
>
> An Identity Theft report is a second kind of report. It is a police report with more detail. To be an Identity Theft report, it should have enough information about the crime that the credit reporting companies and the businesses involved can verify that you're a victim, and know which accounts or information have been affected. It's the report that will give you access to many of the rights described here.
>
> The FTC's Identity Theft complaint form is a good place to start documenting the theft of your Identity. This form asks you for the kind of detail that the Identity Theft report requires. Once you fill out this form online and print it, you can use it with the police report to create your Identity Theft report.

Dealing with Credit Reporting Companies

You have the right to:

> ➤ Place a 90-day initial fraud alert on your credit files. You would do this if you think you are — or may become — the victim of Identity Theft. A fraud alert tells users of your credit report that they must take reasonable steps to verify who is applying for credit in your name. To place a 90-day fraud alert, contact just one of the three nationwide credit reporting companies. The one you contact has to notify the other two.

> ➤ Place a seven-year extended fraud alert on your credit files. You would do this if you know you are a victim of Identity Theft. You will need to give an Identity Theft report to each of the credit reporting companies. Each credit reporting company will ask you to give them some way for potential creditors to reach you, like a phone number. They will place this contact information on the extended fraud alert as a signal to those who use your credit report that they must contact you before they can issue credit in your name.

> ➤ Get one free copy of your credit report and a summary of your rights from each credit reporting company. You can get these when you place a 90-day initial fraud alert on your credit

reports. When you place an extended fraud alert with any credit reporting company, you have the right to two copies of that credit report during a 12-month period. These credit reports are in addition to the free credit report that all consumers are entitled to each year.

➤ Ask the credit reporting companies to block fraudulent information from appearing on your credit report. To do this, you must submit a copy of a valid Identity Theft report. The credit reporting companies then must tell any creditors who gave them fraudulent information that it resulted from Identity Theft. The creditors may not then turn the fraudulent debts over to debt collectors.

➤ Dispute fraudulent or inaccurate information on your credit report with a credit reporting company. The credit reporting company must investigate your charges, and fix your report if they find that the information is fraudulent.

Dealing with Creditors, Debt Collectors, and Merchants

You have the right to:

> ➤ Have a credit report free of fraudulent accounts. Once you give creditors and debt collectors a copy of a valid Identity Theft report, they may not report fraudulent accounts to the credit reporting companies.

> ➤ Get copies of documents related to the theft of your Identity — for example, applications used to open new accounts or transaction records — if you give the company a valid police report. You also can tell the company to give the documents to a specific law enforcement agency; that agency doesn't have to get a subpoena for the records.

> ➤ Stop the collection of fraudulent debts. You may ask debt collectors to stop contacting you to collect on fraudulent debts. You also may ask them to give you information related to the debt, like the names of the creditors and the amounts of the debts.

In many states, you have the right to be notified by a business or organization that has lost or misplaced certain types of personal information. Contact your state attorney general's office for more information.

Limiting Your Loss From Identity Theft

Various laws limit your liability for fraudulent debts caused by Identity Theft.

> **Fraudulent Credit Card Charges**: You cannot be held liable for more than $50 for fraudulent purchases made with your credit card, as long as you let the credit card company know within 60 days of when the credit card statement with the fraudulent charges was sent to you. Some credit card issuers say cardholders who are victims of fraudulent transactions on their accounts have no liability for them at all.

> **Lost or Stolen ATM/Debit Card**: If your ATM or debit card is lost or stolen, you may not be held liable for more than $50 for the misuse of your card, as long as you notify the bank or credit union within two business days after you realize the card is missing. If you do not report the loss of your card promptly, your liability may increase.

> **Fraudulent Electronic Withdrawals**: If fraudulent electronic withdrawals are made from your bank or credit union account, and your ATM or debit card has not been lost or stolen, you are not liable, as long as you notify the bank or credit union in writing of the error within 60 days of the date the bank or credit union account

statement with the fraudulent withdrawals was sent to you.

> **Fraudulent Checks**: Under most state laws, you are liable for just a limited amount for fraudulent checks issued on your bank or credit union account, <u>as long as you notify the bank or credit union promptly</u>. Contact your state banking or consumer protection agency for more information.

> **Fraudulent New Accounts**: Under most state laws, you are not liable for any debt incurred on fraudulent accounts opened in your name and without your permission. Contact your state attorney general's office for more information.

Other Federal Rights

Identity Theft victims have other rights when the Identity Thief is being prosecuted in federal court. For example, under the Justice for All Act, the U.S. Department of Justice says Identity Theft victims have the right:

> To be reasonably protected from the accused;

➢ To reasonable, accurate, and timely notice of any public court proceeding, any parole proceeding involving the crime, or any release or escape of the accused;

➢ To not be excluded from any such public court proceeding unless the court determines that the Identity Theft victim's testimony would be materially altered if he or she heard other testimony at that proceeding;

➢ To be reasonably heard at any public proceeding in the district court involving release, plea, sentencing, or any parole proceeding;

➢ To confer with the attorney for the government in the case;

➢ To full and timely restitution as provided by law

➢ To proceedings free from unreasonable delay; and

➢ To be treated with fairness and with respect for his or her dignity and privacy.

Other State Rights

You may have additional rights under state laws. Contact your state attorney general's office to learn more.

Had enough?

<u>Do you feel like this yet?</u>

HOPE

I have been telling you throughout this book that there is HOPE. And, you have arrived where there is hope.

The Marketplace

Over the past several years there have been Identity Theft Protection services popping up like weeds in my father's garden. Be weary of who you do business with. Many- actually most- of these companies, are in fact start-ups. They are touting $1 million dollars of insurance coverage if you are a victim if Identity Theft while under their care. Banks and Insurance companies have also jumped on this bandwagon, offering their own reimbursement coverage.   Some banks go as far as to offer you a dedicated fraud specialist for your case until your credit is restored.

Compare of your options

For the start-up companies, you need to look into who the founders and management are. What is the background of the principles and founders? What kind of experience do the founders and management have in the Identity Theft Arena? What kind of help are they going to be providing when the inevitable happens? Are they offering you an insurance type of protection when you are a victim?   Are you going to be on your own for the restoration? Are the legal expenses on you or are they covered up-front? Have a contract lawyer read the fine print. Will their coverage help or be available to you if you are already a victim?

Head this phrase:

The bold print giveth and the fine print taketh away.

Now that you have read this far, you should be asking: Is that service for credit monitoring only? You will find that credit monitoring is all you get with the start-up services. What about the four other areas where you can be victimized?

When the cold steel hits your wrists for that criminal warrant: "How is credit monitoring going to help you?" It Won't!

You will find that the four other areas are not even addressed.

Some of these start-up services will place pre-emptive fraud alerts on your credit file. You need to think of, how will that affect my family? Do you have children heading off to college? Will they need financial aid? Will you need a new car in the next year or so? Are you considering refinancing your house? The fraud alert will affect not

> In December 2003, the Office of the comptroller of the Currency (OCC) directed a large financial institution to improve its employee screening policies, procedures, systems, and controls after finding that the institution had inadvertently hired a convicted felon who used his new post to engage in Identity Theft related crimes. Deficiencies in the institution's screening practices came to light through the OCC's review of the former employee's activities.

only what a thief may initiate, but what you can or cannot do in your life as well.

Remember we're talking COLD HARD REALITY. Credit monitoring alone, does offer some hope, but is not the best answer.

Banks and Insurance companies would like you to believe that they are your best answer of Hope as well. Some banks as you have already discovered, by reading these pages, don't necessarily have your best interest in mind. Think back, to the Fair Credit Billing Act, did you lobby congress when that legislation was under consideration? I know I didn't. I'm willing to bet that you didn't either. But, the banks did. That is why the regulation reads the way it does. Don't get me wrong. I'm not saying the banks are evil or anything like that. I am currently working with a few small banks to begin offering the same services that I offer, simply, because it makes sense. What I am saying is that you need to consider the options. Most banks are monitoring your credit. They are also telling you that they will provide a dedicated fraud specialist until your credit is restored. Fantastic! What about the lawsuit you're facing from the outstanding hospital bills? Are they going to provide legal council? How about the IRS audit and fines from the lettuce- picking job in Arizona, or the meatpacking job in Arkansas? Again, are they going to provide a Tax attorney for the audit?

I am going to have to give you a resounding NO on those questions. Sorry, Most Banks are not your best answer.

Insurance companies! They have got to be the best answer right?

Wrong!

Insurance companies are offering riders to existing policies you may already have in place. They may offer a stand-alone type of protection as well. These policies or riders have more exclusions than a dryer has socks hidden in it.

Have you ever heard of an Insurance company denying a claim? Hmm… I have.

Do you think that there is a possibility of the Insurance Company denying your claim for your Identity Theft nightmare?

Sorry, not the Best Answer.

Something I haven't even mentioned that applies to all of the above options is: Reimbursement.

All of the above options operate on a reimbursement principle. Meaning: You pay for the expenses associated with the Identity Theft and they will consider paying you back. Expenses you can expect to be paying out-of-pocket can be: faxes, certified mail, bail, postage (priority, maybe overnight), sworn statements, notary fees, attorneys fees, you get the picture. The amount you can expect to pay out-of-pocket can range in the thousands (i.e. $1500-$4,500 excluding attorneys fees). You can also add lost wages to that total.

Example:

The IRS congratulates you with an audit. If it is a serious audit, one of the first things the IRS will do is seize or freeze your bank accounts. How are you supposed to pay out-of-pocket expenses? That is just a question, for you to ponder. It came to my mind and I'm sure it entered yours as well.

Sorry, Reimbursement is not your Best Answer, for HOPE.

TIME

Time is our most valuable asset. As a victim of Identity Theft you are going to consume a lot of time. The FTC says between 600 and 1500 hours. Let's say you only need  10% of that amount of time. You are still looking at

60 to 150 hours of your time. The low end is more than one full workweek. Where are you going to get that much time to handle this situation?
Are you a self-employed type? Your time is literally your livelihood.
With the above options you are on your own for the time commitment.

That is Brutal Reality!

Sorry, Reimbursement, still not the BEST ANSWER.

The average person will look at those options and think they are solid protection. You on the other hand can take a discerning eye toward the shortfalls of those product offerings, since you have begun to educate yourself.

THE BEST ANSWER

I am an:
Identity Theft Risk Management Specialist

I have taken the time to research the various types of Identity Theft products in the marketplace. I obviously offer a protective service. Notice, I said <u>protective service</u>. For the service that I offer visit:

www.OneMillionFamilies.com

Many of the companies in the marketplace call themselves a preventative service. As a reader of this book you know that is not possible. Your information is already out there. Therefore, the only way to prevent is to not have your information out there.

TOO LATE!

Your information is irretrievably out there. So, your only true option at this point is protective measures.

When you are comparing each of the services within the market you need to look for three primary functions from that service.

- ➢ Continuous Identity Monitoring. Not just credit monitoring.

- ➢ Restoration! Not Reimbursement. You want the restoration to be done by Licensed Professionals. Not someone that studied a correspondence course. A kick in the reality would be to contrast the training of your hairdresser/ barber with that of the 'fraud specialists' you talk to on the phone at these start-up companies. The Cold Hard Reality is that the person cutting or styling your hair has more in-depth training than that 'fraud specialist' you are talking with. Restoration also means that you do very little of the work of repairing the damage. The Licensed Professionals handle the bulk of it for you. That alone is empowering.

> Access to Nationwide Legal Council. You are going to need it!

www.OneMillionFamilies.com

The service I represent cannot prevent Identity Theft. NO SERVICE CAN!! The service I represent can and does serve as your early warning system. Would you agree that it is better to detect cancer earlier than later? My time is extremely valuable to me. Restoration, and access to nationwide legal council was a MUST HAVE for any service that I was going to attach my Identity to.
OK. That was my commercial. I obviously feel very strongly about the products that I represent. Visit

www.OneMillionFamilies.com

Then you'll understand why for yourself.

Final Thoughts

Now you know. There is more to the Identity Theft pandemic than you may have first thought or been lead to believe. You have read some examples and scenarios of what the Cold Hard Reality of Identity Theft really is. These examples and scenarios were sanitized (read as not the worst case scenarios, or most nightmarish) to keep from totally freaking you out, yet they are real and the reality of Identity Theft. You probably had heard the numbers of Identity Theft victims before. Understanding what those numbers comprise was the mystery. Now you Know.

I encourage you to take action from here. Enroll in a program that can provide true protective services for you and your family.

Whether you choose, to go with the service I have aligned myself with or not, doesn't matter to me. My clients have gone with the best answer for their family.

My intent with this book has been to give you an introductory level education on Identity Theft and the options available to you. You need to continue this education on your own. There are two basic ways to continue your education:

- One is through trial and error as the stumbling victim. Committing to all of the steps and measures outlined in the 'Going it ALONE' section

- The other way to continue your education is with experts on your side, as the empowered, confident person you are.

Comparative Breakdown:

- 'Going it ALONE' **Vs.** Start-Up Company **Vs.** My Service offering of 60+ years combined Experience between the two Companies I am aligned with.

- 'Going it ALONE' **Vs.** Credit Monitoring **Vs.** My Service Offering of Identity Monitoring with Licensed Fraud Investigators.

- 'Going it ALONE' or with a Start-Up Company (same as Going it ALONE) committing 600/1500 hours of your time **Vs.** Less than 10 hours of your time with My Service Offering.

- 'Going it ALONE' **Vs.** Reimbursement **Vs.** Restoration with My Service Offering.

As an expert in the Identity Theft arena, I know my clients have gone with the Best Answer for their family.

My Service offering:www.OneMillionFamilies.com

Acknowledgments

First of all I want to thank my Mother, Carrie, and Father, Jack, for their incredible guidance and love in my life. Without my parents strong Christian upbringing I know I wouldn't be at the point I am at in my life. I can never express it enough: I Love You!

My Sisters, Faith and Tammy. Even with all, of the sibling differences growing up you have never lost confidence in me. Love you both! Thank you.

Valreen. You are the true love of my life, the final love of my life. I want to grow very old with you. I Love you forever!

Uncle Mike. More like an older brother than an uncle. Your confidence and encouragement have kept me going long past the points where I wanted to give up. Understood yet never expressed, Love You.

All of my family: Aunts, Uncles, Cousins, niece, and nephew. Each one of you individually would be a book in itself. Thank you.

Many mentors in my life have said that you are the sum total of the five people you spend the most time with. Well, I am the sum total of hundreds of people. Thank you, to all of you. Some mentors I have never met face to face, but you all have impacted my life. At the peril of missing some of you, I apologize.

Harland Stonecipher, Pre-Paid Legal Services Inc., Wilburn Smith, Greg Haus, Jim Harkema, Kathy Aaron, Ann and Jessie Alford, Kim Miljus, Holly Stevens, Gloria Sawyer, Ann Palmer, Ronnie and Shelia King, Melia Family, Jim Chandler, Frank and Theresa Aucoin, Mick Coons, Ted Wilson, Dr. David Powers, Dr. Angela and Tim Peery, Chuck and Martha Govey, Rob, Suzanne, Steve, Larry and Monica Moore, Shauna, Jeremy, Sharon, Jim Rohn, Caroline, Nancy, Don Foor, Gribbons, Darulas, John Drennan, Hills, Dr. Tom and Wanda Cooke, Ron and Becky Salvino, Michele Shannon, Al Jackson, Dave Savula, Chuck Wagner, Jeff Olsen, Phil and Mary Smarrella, Brian and Cheryl Smarrella, Kevin and Melissa McGrath, John Gardner, Rick Gunter, Benjamine Creel, Jim Stevens, Blakely Cahoun, Bob DeLoach, Tom McDermott, Ben and Kerri Crauder, Chris and Sarah Malloch, Chris and Madeline Elswick, Marion and Michele Moore, Lee and Suzanne Kelley, Tricia Fielden, Rob and Jackie Peeden, Kristen Grace, Joyce Suliman, Lester and Monna Blankenship, Rick and Kathy Embrey, Shannon Sweeney, Sharon Bailey, Chris and Nan Trout, Donna Kouril, Lori Stifter, Darren Squires, James Blackmon, Darren Taylor, Iceman, Mixin Dixon, Veronica DeMay, Renee Wikstrom, Woody Sellers, Dr James E Madory, Ted Rawley, Nick Terezis, Ray Olivi, Scott Madory, All United States Marines Past-Present-and Future Semper Fi, The entire SECRET CREW.

Keeping the Lawyers Happy

The author of this book is not an attorney, nor is it to be inferred, implied or assumed as such. No information contained within this book is to be viewed, considered, or interpreted as legal advice.

This publication is designed to provide general information regarding the subject matter covered. The author has taken reasonable measures and precautions in the presentation of this material and believes all of the information contained herein is true and accurate as of the time it was written. Some information may have changed since publishing. Identity Theft is an Evolving Crime; therefore laws and procedures must evolve with the crime. Be sure to utilize the resources provided herein to obtain the most current guidelines and procedures. The author and publisher disclaim any liability resulting from use or application of the information contained herein.

The services the author provides vary from state to state and province to province. Some exclusions, variations, and licensing may apply for your state or province. The author may not have license privileges for your state or province. The author does have business associates in your state or province that can assist you for your protection. For more comprehensive details and explanations of such exclusions and a licensed associate in your state or province contact the author at:

author@IdentityTheft-Reality.com

In your E-mail please provide your name, best method of contact (i.e. E-mail, phone: C-H-W), your home state or province, and of course your name.

RESOURCES
STATISTICS

---

www.OneMillionFamilies.com

www.IdentityTheft-Reality.com
    This books homepage. Containing: additional
    links, resources, and action step checklists.

These are additional resources to the extensive listing
above.

www.privacyrights.org
www.idtheftcenter.org
www.ftc.gov
www.idtheft.gov
www.ssa.gov
www.transunion.com
www.exuifax.com
www.experian.com
www.annualcreditreport.com
www.financialprivacynow.org

Statistics

- _**Identity Theft Complaints**_
- **[Fraud Complaints]**

(In thousands)

CY-2004	CY-2005	CY-2006
657,591	**693,519**	**674,354**
_246,882_	_255,613_	_246,035_
[410,709]	**[437,906]**	**[428,319]**

Federal Trade Commission Released February 7, 2007

Top Complaint Categories[1]

January 1 – December 31, 2006

Federal Trade Commission Released February 7, 2007

Rank Top Categories Complaints Percentage[1]

1 Identity Theft 246,035 36%
2 Shop-at-Home/Catalog Sales 46,995 7%
3 Prizes/Sweepstakes and Lotteries 45,587 7%
4 Internet Services and Computer Complaints 41,243 6%
5 Internet Auctions 32,832 5%
6 Foreign Money Offers 20,411 3%
7 Advance-Fee Loans and Credit Protection/Repair 10,857 2%
8 Magazines and Buyers Clubs 8,924 1%
9 Telephone Services 8,165 1%
10 Health Care 7,467 1%
11 Business Opps and Work-at-Home Plans 7,460 1%
12 Travel, Vacations and Timeshare 6,712 1%
13 Office Supplies and Services 5,723 1%
14 Grants: Scholarships/Educational & Non-Educational 5,310 1%
15 Employ Agencies/Job Counsel/Overseas Work 4,485 1%
16 Investments 3,630 1%
Other Coded Complaints 12,399 2%

1 Percentages are based on the total number of Sentinel complaints (674,354) received by the FTC between January 1 and December 31, 2006. Twenty-four percent (160,399) of the Sentinel complaints received by the FTC did not contain specific product service codes.

Identity Theft Complaints by Victim Age[1]

January 1 – December 31, 2006

Under 18	18-29	30-39	40-49	50-59	60 and Over
5%	**29%**	**23%**	**20%**	**13%**	**10%**
					4%
					(60-64)
					6%
					(65 And Over)

[1] Percentages are based on the total number of Identity Theft complaints where victims reported their age (225,532). 94% of the victims who contacted the FTC directly reported their age. *Federal Trade Commission Released February 7, 2007*

Largest Metropolitan Areas Ranking for Identity Theft Consumer Complaints[1]

January 1 – December 31, 2006 Federal Trade Commission Released February 7, 2007

Rank Metropolitan Area Complaints Per 100,000 Population

1 Napa, CA Metro. Statistical Area 403 304.5
2 Madera, CA Metro. Statistical Area 394 283.6
3 McAllen-Edinburg-Mission, TX Metro. Statistical Area 1,693 257.2
4 Greeley, CO Metro. Statistical Area 537 244.9
5 Yuba City, CA Metro. Statistical Area 358 236.5
6 Brownsville-Harlingen, TX Metro. Statistical Area 873 234.8
7 Hanford-Corcoran, CA Metro. Statistical Area 324 227.3
8 Albany-Lebanon, OR Micropolitan Statistical Area 230 214.1
9 Vallejo-Fairfield, CA Metro. Statistical Area 875 211.9
10 Laredo, TX Metro. Statistical Area 464 211.4
11 Flagstaff, AZ Metro. Statistical Area 257 209.4
12 Thomasville-Lexington, NC Micropolitan Statistical Area 301 195.7
13 Prescott, AZ Metro. Statistical Area 354 185.7
14 Sierra Vista-Douglas, AZ Micropolitan Statistical Area 229 184.7
15 Gainesville, GA Metro. Statistical Area 297 184.6
16 Lake Havasu City-Kingman, AZ Micropolitan Statistical Area 319 177.2
17 Phoenix-Mesa-Scottsdale, AZ Metro. Statistical Area 6,533 175.8
18 Monroe, MI Metro. Statistical Area 267 175.0
19 Dunn, NC Micropolitan Statistical Area 177 174.3
20 Tucson, AZ Metro. Statistical Area 1,573 173.4
21 Yuma, AZ Metro. Statistical Area 304 172.6
22 Stockton, CA Metro. Statistical Area 1,118 172.0
23 Bakersfield, CA Metro. Statistical Area 1,245 169.4
24 Las Cruces, NM Metro. Statistical Area 298 160.1
25 Fresno, CA Metro. Statistical Area 1,386 159.9
26 Modesto, CA Metro. Statistical Area 774 155.3
27 Vero Beach, FL Metro. Statistical Area 183 147.4
28 Oxnard-Thousand Oaks-Ventura, CA Metro. Statistical Area 1,176 147.4
29 Corpus Christi, TX Metro. Statistical Area 603 147.2
30 Merced, CA Metro. Statistical Area 347 146.4
31 Riverside-San Bernardino-Ontario, CA Metro. Statistical Area 5,536 145.9
32 Durham, NC Metro. Statistical Area 657 145.6
33 Port St. Lucie-Fort Pierce, FL Metro. Statistical Area 529 145.0
34 Las Vegas-Paradise, NV Metro. Statistical Area 2,376 143.9
35 Hammond, LA Micropolitan Statistical Area 150 142.6
36 Macon, GA Metro. Statistical Area 325 142.4
37 Miami-Ft Lauderdale-Miami Beach, FL Metro. Statistical Area 7,557 140.9
38 Ann Arbor, MI Metro. Statistical Area 478 140.9
39 Salisbury, NC Micropolitan Statistical Area 189 140.7
40 Santa Cruz-Watsonville, CA Metro. Statistical Area 351 140.0
41 Visalia-Porterville, CA Metro. Statistical Area 558 139.0
42 Goldsboro, NC Metro. Statistical Area 158 138.3
43 Yakima, WA Metro. Statistical Area 314 137.1
44 Roseburg, OR Micropolitan Statistical Area 140 135.7
45 Lakeland, FL Metro. Statistical Area 705 134.4

Largest Metropolitan Areas Ranking for Identity Theft Consumer Complaints1... Contd.

January 1 – December 31, 2006 Federal Trade
Commission Released February 7, 2007
Rank Metropolitan Area Complaints Per 100,000 Population

46 Olympia, WA Metro. Statistical Area 301 134.0
47 Dallas-Fort Worth-Arlington, TX Metro. Statistical Area 7,594 133.2
48 Niles-Benton Harbor, MI Metro. Statistical Area 216 132.4
49 Sacramento-Arden-Arcade--Roseville, CA Metro. Statistical Area 2,667 132.2
50 South Bend-Mishawaka, IN-MI Metro. Statistical Area 420 132.0

1Ranking is based on the number of Identity Theft complaints per 100,000 inhabitants for each Metro. Area. This chart illustrates the top 50 Metro. Areas (Metro. and Micropolitan Statistical Areas) with a population of one hundred thousand or more. Metro. Areas presented here are those defined by the Office of Management and Budget as of November 2004 www.census.gov/population/www/estimates/metropop/table01.xls).

Identity Theft Victims by State (Per 100,000 Population) [1]

January 1 – December 31, 2006
Federal Trade Commission Released February 7, 2007

State Ranking/ Victims Per 100,000 Population:

1 Arizona 147.8 9,113
2 Nevada 120.0 2,994
3 California 113.5 41,396
4 Texas 110.6 26,006
5 Florida 98.3 17,780
6 Colorado 92.5 4,395
7 Georgia 86.3 8,084
8 New York 85.2 16,452
9 Washington 83.4 5,336
10 New Mexico 82.9 1,621
11 Maryland 82.9 4,656
12 Illinois 78.6 10,080
13 Oregon 76.1 2,815
14 New Jersey 73.3 6,394
15 Virginia 67.2 5,137
16 Michigan 67.2 6,784

17 Delaware 66.7 569
18 Connecticut 65.8 2,305
19 Pennsylvania 64.9 8,080
20 North Carolina 64.9 5,748
21 Missouri 64.2 3,753
22 Massachusetts 63.7 4,102
23 Oklahoma 63.0 2,254
24 Indiana 62.2 3,928
25 Utah 61.8 1,577
26 Tennessee 61.3 3,700
27 Alabama 60.3 2,774
28 Ohio 59.9 6,878
29 Kansas 58.8 1,626
30 Rhode Island 57.6 615
31 Alaska 57.3 384
32 South Carolina 55.7 2,408
33 Minnesota 55.6 2,872
34 Arkansas 54.7 1,537
35 Louisiana 52.6 2,256
36 Mississippi 51.3 1,494
37 Nebraska 49.1 868
38 Idaho 49.0 718
39 Hawaii 47.8 615
40 New Hampshire 46.1 606
41 Montana 45.9 434
42 Wisconsin 45.6 2,536
43 Wyoming 42.3 218
44 Kentucky 42.0 1,766
45 Maine 39.7 525
46 West Virginia 39.3 715
47 Iowa 34.9 1,041
48 South Dakota 30.2 236
49 North Dakota 29.7 189

50 Vermont 28.5 178

1 Per 100,000 units of population estimates are based on the 2006 U.S. Census population estimates (Table NST-EST2006-01 - Annual Estimates of the Population for the United States and States, and for Puerto Rico: April 1, 2000 to July 1, 2006). Numbers for the District of Columbia are 765 victims and 131.5 victims per 100,000 population.

Credit Reporting Agency (CRA) Contact[1]

Federal Trade Commission Released February 7, 2007

42% of Victims Contacted a CRA and Were Able to Place a Fraud Alert

57% of Victims Had Not Contacted Any CRA

1Percentages are based on the total number of Identity Theft complaints where victims indicated whether they had notified any CRA (233,219). 98% of the victims who contacted the FTC directly reported this information. Note that less than one percent of victims who reported contacting a CRA were unable to place a fraud alert or did not indicate if a fraud alert was placed.
Federal Trade Commission Released February 7, 2007

Law Enforcement Contact [1]

January 1 – December 31, 2006

Federal Trade Commission Released February 7, 2007

62% of Victims Did Not Notify a Police Department

8% of Victims Notified a Police Department and a Report Was NOT Taken

30% of Victims Notified a Police Department and a Report Was Taken

1Percentages are based on the total number of Identity Theft complaints where victims indicated whether they had notified a police department (233,509). 98% of the Identity Theft victims who contacted the FTC directly reported law enforcement contact information. Less than one percent of victims who informed the FTC that they had contacted a police department did not indicate if a report was taken.

Identity Theft Task Force Members

Alberto R. Gonzales, Chairman
Attorney General

Deborah Platt Majoras, Co-Chairman
Chairman, Federal Trade Commission

Henry M. Paulson
Department of Treasury

Carlos M. Gutierrez
Department of Commerce

Michael O. Leavitt
Department of Health and Human Services

R. James Nicholson
Department of Veterans Affairs

Michael Chertoff
Department of Homeland Security

Rob Portman
Office of Management and Budget

John E. Potter
United States Postal Service

Ben S. Bernanke
Federal Reserve System

Linda M. Springer
Office of Personnel Management

Sheila C. Bair
Federal Deposit Insurance Corporation

Christopher Cox
Securities and Exchange Commission

JoAnn Johnson
National Credit Union Administration

Michael J. Astrue
Social Security Administration

John C. Dugan
Office of the Comptroller of the Currency

John M. Reich
Office of Thrift Supervision

State Credit Freeze Guide

STATE:	FEES:	ELIGIBILITY:	EFFECTIVE DATE:	NOTES:
Alabama	-	-	-	-
Alaska	-	-	-	-
Arizona	-	-	-	-
Arkansas	$10.00	IDT Victims	1-Jan-08	$10.00 fee applies for lifting or removing as well
California	Free*	All Consumers	1-Jan-03	Free for IDT Victims. $10.00 all others. $12.00 for temporary lift
Colorado	Free*	All Consumers	1-Jul-06	Free for first Freeze. $10.00 subsequent. $12.00 temp lift for Specific Creditor. $10 lift or remove
Connecticut	$10.00*	All Consumers	1-Jan-06	$10 applies to all general transactions. $12 to lift for a specific creditor.
Delaware	Free*	All Consumers	28-Sep-06	Free for IDT Victims. $20.00 for all others. No fee to remove or lift.
District of Columbia	Free*	All Consumers	1-Jul-07	Free for IDT Victims. $10 all others. No fee to lift or remove.
Florida	Free*	All Consumers	1-Jul-06	Free for IDT Victims and Seniors 65 and over. $10 all others for each transaction.
Georgia	Free*	All Consumers		
Hawaii	Free*	All Consumers	15-Jun-07	Free for IDT Victims. $5 all others for each transaction.
Idaho	-	-	-	-

State Credit Freeze Guide Cont.

STATE:	FEES:	ELIGIBILITY:	EFFECTIVE DATE:	NOTES:
Illinois	Free*	All Consumers	1-Jan-07	Free for IDT Victims W/ Police Report, and 65 and over. $10 all others for each transaction.
Indiana	Free*	All Consumers	1-Sep-07	As of this writing it is free for all consumers.
Iowa		All Consumers		
Kansas	Free*	All Consumers	1-Jan-07	As of this writing it is free for all consumers.
Kentucky	Free*	All Consumers	11-Jul-07	Free for IDT Victims W/ Police Report. $10 all others for each transaction. Freeze Expires. After 7 years.
Louisiana	Free* $8-$10	IDT Victims All Consumers		Free for IDT Victims, and 62 and over. $10 to place freeze. $8 to lift it. No Fee to remove it.
Maine	Free* $10-$12	IDT Victims All Consumers	1-Feb-06	Free for victims with police report. $10 for consumers to place, lift, or remove. $10 for reissue of PIN. $12 to lift for a specific creditor.
Maryland	Free* $5	IDT Victims All Consumers	1-Jan-08 1-Jan-08	Free for victims who give report of alleged Identity Fraud or an Identity Theft Passport. $5 all other for each transaction.
Massachusetts	-	-	-	-
Michigan	-	-	-	-
Minnesota	Free*	All Consumers	1-Aug-06	Free for Victims with report. $5 all others
Mississippi	$10	IDT Victims	1-Aug-06	$10 IDT Victims with Police Report or complaint filed.
Missouri	-	-	-	-

138

State Credit Freeze Guide Cont.

STATE:	FEES:	ELIGIBILITY:	EFFECTIVE DATE:	NOTES:
	Free*	IDT Victims		Free for IDT Victims. $3 to place or lift freeze. $5 for PIN reissue. No fee to remove freeze.
Montana	$3-$5	All Consumers	1-Jul-07	
Nebraska	Free*	IDT Victims		Free for IDT Victims. $15 to place the freeze. No fee to lift or remove the freeze. Freeze auto expires after 7 years.
	$15	All Consumers	1-Sep-08	
Nevada	Free*	IDT Victims		Free for IDT Victims who submit police report. All others $15 to place. $18 to lift or remove. $20 to lift for Specific creditor.
	$15-$20	All Consumers	1-Oct-05	
New Hampshire	Free*	IDT Victims		Free for IDT Victims that file police report or similar documentation. $10 All others for each action.
	$10	All Consumers	1-Jan-07	
New Jersey	Free/ $5	All Consumers	1-Jan-06	Free for first freeze. $5 to lift or remove the freeze, or to reissue PIN. Can make requests directly to CRA via Secure electronic mail.
New Mexico	Free*	IDT Victims		Free for IDT Victims with Police Report. Or 65 and over. $10 all other to place freeze. $5 to lift or remove.
	$5-$10	All Consumers	1-Jul-07	
New York	Free/ $5	All Consumers	1-Nov-06	Free for IDT Victims and first time placement. $5 for non-victims to lift or remove it. Reinstate freeze $5.
North Carolina	Free*	IDT Victims		IDT Victims Free with valid police report or similar documentation. $10 for all others for each transaction.
	$10	All Consumers	1-Dec-05	
North Dakota	Free*	IDT Victims		IDT Victims Free with valid police report or similar documentation. $5 for all others to place or lift. No fee to remove.
	$5	All Consumers	1-Jul-07	
Ohio	-	-	-	-

State Credit Freeze Guide Cont.

STATE:	FEES:	ELIGIBILITY:	EFFECTIVE DATE:	NOTES:
Oklahoma	Free*	IDT Victims 65	1-Jan-07	Free for IDT Victims with Police report or 65 an over. $10 all others for each transaction.
	$10	All Consumers		
Oregon	-	-	-	-
Pennsylvania	Free*	IDT Victims 65	1-Jan-07	Free for IDT Victims or 65 and over. $10 all other to place or lift. No fee to remove.
	$10	All Consumers		
Rhode Island	Free*	IDT Victims 65	1-Jan-07	Free for IDT victims and 65 or over. $10 all others for each transaction.
	$10	All Consumers		
South Carolina	-	-	-	-
South Dakota	Free*	All Consumers	1-Jul-06	Only freezes Credit Report. Auto expires after 7 years.
Tennessee	Free*	All Consumers	1-Jan-08	Free for IDT Victims. $5-$7.50 all others.
Texas	Free	IDT Victims	1-Sep-03	Free for IDT Victims. $10 all others for each transaction, except $12 to Temp. lift for a specific creditor.
	$10-$12	All Consumers	1-Sep-07	
Utah	*	All Consumers	1-Sep-08	*Credit Bureaus can charge 'Reasonable Fees'. Can 'Thaw' or Lift the Freeze within 15 minutes of an electronic request.
Vermont	Free*	All Consumers	1-Jul-06	Free for IDT Victims. $10 to Freeze. $5 all others for each transaction.
Virginia	-	-	-	-
Washington	*	IDT Victims	**	*Currently Available and Free for IDT Victims and Seniors 65. ** 1-July-2008 $10 all consumers, for each transaction.
West Virginia	Free*	All Consumers	2-Jul-07	Free for IDT Victims. $5 all others for each transaction.

State Credit Freeze Guide Cont.

Wisconsin	Free*	All Consumers	1-Jan-07	Free for IDT Victims, with proof of victimization. $10 all others for each transaction.
Wyoming	Free*	All Consumers	1-Jul-07	Free for IDT Victims. $10 all others.

Note: Each transaction means for each action you as the consumer take regarding your credit freeze. Many states have not passed legislation pertaining to credit freezes for the citizens of those states. Check with your states Attorney General office for upcoming Identity Theft laws. You can find links to your Attorney Generals website at:

www.IdentityTheft-Reality.com

NOTES